HOLIDAYS AND FESTIVALS

Thanksgiving

Rebecca Rissman

Heinemann Library
Chicago, Illinois

www.heinemannraintree.com
Visit our website to find out
more information about
Heinemann-Raintree books.

To order:

☎ Phone 888-454-2279

💻 Visit www.heinemannraintree.com
to browse our catalog and order online.

Edited by Adrian Vigliano and Rebecca Rissman
Designed by Ryan Frieson
Picture research by Tracy Cummins
Leveling by Nancy E. Harris
Originated by Capstone Global Library Ltd.
Printed in China by South China Printing Company Ltd.

15 14 13 12 11 10
10 9 8 7 6 5 4 3 2 1

Library of Congress Cataloging-in-Publication Data
Rissman, Rebecca.
  Thanksgiving / Rebecca Rissman.
     p. cm.—(Holidays and festivals)
  Includes bibliographical references and index.
  ISBN 978-1-4329-4058-4 (hc)—ISBN 978-1-4329-4077-5 (pb) 1.
Thanksgiving Day—Juvenile literature. I. Title.
  GT4975.R57 2011
  394.2649—dc22

2009052858

Acknowledgments

The author and publishers are grateful to the following for permission to
reproduce copyright material: Corbis ©SHANNON STAPLETON/Reuters
p.5; Corbis ©Trolley Dodger **p.11**; Corbis ©Bettmann **p.13**; Corbis
©Randy Faris **p.14**; Corbis ©Bettmann **p.23b**; Corbis ©SHANNON
STAPLETON/Reuters **p.23d**; Getty Images/SuperStock **p.8**; Getty
Images **p.9**; Getty Images/Judd Pilossof **p.15**; Getty Images/White
Packert **p.16**; Getty Images/Angus Williams **p.17**; istockphoto ©Wesley
Pohl **p.18**; istockphoto ©Lee Pettet **p.21**; istockphoto ©John Clines
p.22; istockphoto ©Lee Pettet **p.23a**; Photolibrary/Ariel Skelley **p.4**;
Photolibrary/Ryan McVay **p.19**; Shutterstock ©Jeff Banke **p.20**; The
Granger Collection, New York **pp.6**, **7**, **10**, **12**, **23c**.

Cover photograph of hands holding whole roasted Thanksgiving turkey
on platter reproduced with permission of Getty Images/Lew Robertson.
Back cover photograph reproduced with permission of Shutterstock
©Jeff Banke.

Every effort has been made to contact copyright holders of any material
reproduced in this book. Any omissions will be rectified in subsequent
printings if notice is given to the publisher.

Contents

What Is a Holiday?

A holiday is a special day.
People celebrate holidays.

Thanksgiving is a holiday.
Thanksgiving is in November.

The Story of Thanksgiving

The pilgrims were a group of people who came to America from England.

The pilgrims had very hard lives.

One winter was very cold. Many pilgrims died. Then people called

the Wampanoag came to help.

The Wampanoag were Indians who had lived on the land for many years.

The Wampanoag taught the pilgrims to farm.

The Wampanoag taught the pilgrims to fish and hunt.

The pilgrims were thankful for what
the Wampanoag had taught them.

The pilgrims had a big meal to celebrate the harvest. Many people say this was the first Thanksgiving meal.

Celebrating Thanksgiving

On Thanksgiving people eat a big meal called a feast.

Many people eat turkey, stuffing, and pie. But any food can be part of the feast.

On Thanksgiving people watch sports and parades.

People play games and talk.

On Thanksgiving people spend time with family and friends.

People remember to be thankful for what they have.

Thanksgiving Symbols

The turkey is a symbol of Thanksgiving.

The cornucopia is a symbol
of Thanksgiving.

Calendar

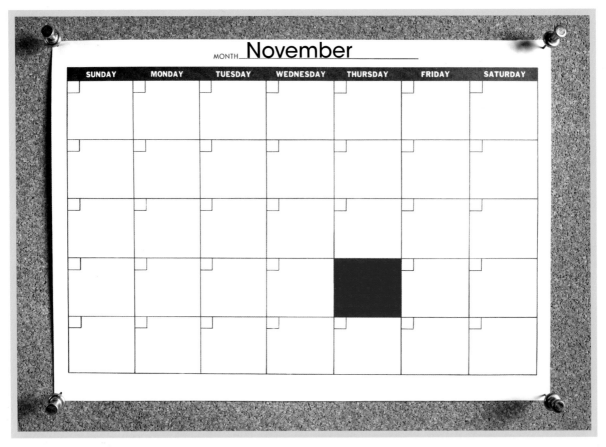

Thanksgiving is the fourth Thursday of November.

Picture Glossary

 **cornucopia** a basket shaped like a horn that is full of food

 **harvest** the time when farmers can gather food they have grown

 **pilgrims** group of people who traveled from England to live in America

 **parade** group of people marching together to celebrate something

Index

Note to Parents and Teachers

Before reading
Explain that every November Americans celebrate Thanksgiving. Ask the children to share their thoughts on the holiday. Do they have stories or memories to share? How does their family celebrate? Ask the children to think about something for which they are thankful.

After reading
Make a "giving thanks" mural. Using butcher paper, create a large canvas. Ask each child to illustrate in pictures and/or words something for which they are thankful. Hang in the classroom and pick one or two items a day to share with the group.